Where Well-Meaning And Broken Men Go

benita peele

Made with ❤ on the BookLeaf Publishing Platform

www.bookleafpub.in

www.bookleafpub.com

Dedication

in memory of zach peele

Preface

On May 10th, 2024, I lost a light brighter than I've ever known. Zachary Peele was an outstanding father, husband, brother, and son. He worked tirelessly to advocate for the recovery of those who struggle with mental health and addiction. He was a selfless, caring husband, and the person I feared losing most in this world. Inside is a 21-day look into my grief. Inside, you will find a different sense of this loss with every day that passes. I am writing this in the hopes that I will reach others who are grieving, so that we may know that we are not alone in the face of catastrophic loss.

Acknowledgements

to alyssa, for encouraging me every step of the way

and meg, for the cover and the unconditional love

1. wedding ring

i know it's here somewhere.
its light glinted
from this spot
as i walked out
of the room.
so i know it's here.
it's not on
the table,
or in the corners
or drawers
but please god,
let it still be here.
i can't lose it.
i think I heard
it fall
when i left
so it must be in this room.
it's just
where all the pens
and hairties go.
still, how could i have left
something so precious
in a position
so precarious?

i think i just
have to lay in this room
until it turns up.

i know
he's here somewhere.
he was in the kitchen
as i fell asleep,
so i know he's here.
he's not at his desk
or with the kids
or in our bed
but please god,
let him be here.
i can't lose him.
i heard his whispered
"i love you"
as i fell asleep.
he's gotta be with us
somewhere,
in the place
well meaning and broken men
go.
why couldn't i have just
gotten out of bed
to tell him i loved him
too?

i think i just
have to lay here
until he walks back
into this room.

i know he's home.
but when i find him
i'll etch his name on a stone
and lay it
where the loved and the lost go.

2. unfathomable

could you
watch your world burn
and gather what
what precious little
remained
as the smoke parted?

could you imagine
the weight of the cinders
piling atop your shoulders
forcing
those beautiful things
from your arms?

can you see yourself
waking each morning
still covered
in burns
with only scars
to look forward to?

you might picture
the disaster relief
desperately

gathering the material
to rebuild.
you may realize
that they will never replace
the hope.

you might imagine yourself
scrounging the strength
to stand firm against
the smell
of a smothered flame.
you might think
your sinew grows
strong enough
to pick up the pieces.

but all you know
is who you are
before the blaze.

3. symbiotic

i laid under
the clouds
and marveled at the
wisteria vine
wrapped around
the branches
of a dying oak.

to my horror,
i began to imagine
myself
the tree
suffocating
as the parasite took root
from trunk to branches
where roots
clung to
her bark
and hid blood
with blossoms.

rest assured
the wisteria
one day

would run out
of life
to take
and wither away
alongside her leaves.

some days it hurt
to lay in your arms.

4. in pieces

i'll leave a light on
until you come home
and wait awake
for your embrace

i'll stare at the
empty seat
at the dinner table
hoping to hear
your laugh.

i'll search for
our rhythm
in the worst
of men
knowing the best of them
are still empty.

i'll say
your mourning prayers
and wait for a sign
that you hold the peace
you traded for mine

i'll lay down and die
through holidays
and first steps
but force your smile
onto my face.
i cannot find mine
anymore.

i'll wear my grief
a blanket wrapped
around my shoulders
shivering
with every attempt
to shrug it off.

if you ever leave me
know you could not leave
any piece
untouched.

5. forest fire

she sat me down
ocean eyes to brown mist,
and told me
of forest fires.
every summer,
as the sun
dried the earth
flames tore through
the brush
reaping life
from all beholden to
its light.
all that is left behind
are ashes.

i expected next
to be compared
a phoenix
and prepared to
remind her
i do not
have the strength
of legends.

i am buried under
the weight
of this cinder.
but under
the soot-colored blanket
are seeds.
she insists
the ashes
will nurture them.
saplings will emerge.
slowly
but not without further death
the forest will be
reborn.

i am buried
under the weight
of this cinder.
i grasp her hands
and beg her for rain.

6. zero sum game

i promised
not to keep score.
sometimes a union
takes from those within.
you vowed that we
would be a zero-sum game.
some days
loving you
was bloodletting,
life spilling
from my body
for the hope
of good health.
but it made a family.
i wonder if you went
knowing every drop
spilled
was worth it.

some days
loving me was
the impossible weight
of your body
as toddler giggles

pulled you out of bed.
but it made
the levity
i knew
our home to be.
i wonder if you laid down
your head at night
knowing your strength
held me up too.

7. reflection

i do not know this woman.
her legs quiver with every step.
her eyes are too swollen
to recognize the disaster
lurking in her path.

i do not know her.
she fills novels with longing
but cannot hold tightly
to those who remain.
this effete
shell of a woman.
she screams prayers
meant for someone else's mouth.

she is estranged
from the person i once knew.
there should seen herself
a heroine,
no matter
how bruised.
the woman in my mirror
instead
shatters.

she should have pulled
from within
a mother, a daughter,
a sister, a friend.
she cannot even find
a self.

8. horizon

you're out
discovering
what it's like
out where the ocean
touches the sky.
i am watching from the shore
nursing a clandestine
wish
that the wind bites you
the same way
it stings me.
how beautiful
the sun
that sears me
must be
when it rises above you.
how amusing it must be
to watch me
swim after
the horizon.
i hope
when i begin to drown
you claw at the heavens
knowing

unlike the stars
and the sea
you and i
are never again
to meet.

9. daughter

he never comes home
empty-handed.
when dada gets back,
he'll bring me lollipops.
he'll put me
on his shoulders
and dance.
he'll tell me he missed me
so much.
he'll take me outside
and we'll make wishes
on dandelions
and let ladybugs
crawl on our hands.
mama tells me heaven
is too far away.
i know my dada
is just looking
for the biggest lollipop
out there.

10. on a good day

she lies atop a blanket
by the water
to stare up at the clouds
and for just a little while
forget about
the ground below her.

at first, the hiss is so quiet
she is not sure
that she heard it.
it becomes
decidedly
too pronounced
to ignore.

she is staring down
a water moccasin.
it has remained still
for far longer than
one naturally would.
she calls it mercy.

it would chase her if
if she even breathed

in the wrong direction.
it would approach her
if she stayed still
long enough.
she imagines
the pinpricks and
fading vision
to come.

she lies atop a blanket
by the water
to stare up at the clouds
and for just a little while
forget about
the ground below her.

11. the invisible panes

the warmth
of your hands
meets a cool panel,
your words of comfort
garbled behind it.
i accept
gifts
as i would
candles and flowers
at my gravesite.

it may be because
during the snowstorm
i was buried in ice
and fossilized.
perhaps i am
now set
behind four glass panes,
marveled at and mourned for,
a collection of bones
with no recollection
of she who withered away.

your grasp

could never quite
have reached me.

12. holiday

dear zachy,

it's christmas
and hanukkah eve.
thank you for the snow.
i took our daughter
to the park by the
grocery store.
we made
the mini snowman again
with
the baby carrot
nose.
she told me she wishes
she could build it with you.

i tore myself apart
debating
whether or not
to write "from dada"
on her presents.

she asked me
if santa comes from heaven.

as she laid down
she asked
if he saw you
and if we can go too.
i wept over her sleeping frame.

we got a tree
and a menorah.
one for each of us.
i'll say your prayers
and light your candles
and wonder if i
did you justice.

I will leave an empty seat
at dinner
and stare at it
waiting for your jokes and smiles.

i love you.
i will never stop seeing
the space where you should be.

love,
benita

13. holding space

we once fled from
a sinkhole
together
and found ourselves
sheltering from the
desolation
in the same room.
i leaned into the wall
and became a mirror
to your grief.

those eyes were once
in my reflection.
you once pressed your hand
onto the cold glass
of my body.

as the longing fades
and my temperature
starts to permeate
into your fingers
you withdraw your touch
and gasping from the cold
take a step away.

this room stops being home
to you.
your figure
in this mirror
shrinks with each step
and disappears.

you're brave enough
to leave the room.
i am left
once again
in the empty space.

14. the hardest days

the hardest days
are the ones with the smiles.
they're supposed to
suffuse
from children's squeals
and grandfather's pride.
they're supposed to come
from the
snowman
built in two inches
of melting snow.
but smiles
for this season
are carved
with sickles
and expectation.

the hardest days
are the ones you made
the biggest.
the ones I light candles for
where you once lit
fireworks.
the ones where i knead dough

unfamiliar to my hands
and sing
with joy that
no longer fits
in my throat.

the hardest days
are the ones
in which collapsing,
tears,
disappearing into
your shadow
are the biggest sins.
the ones
in which
tradition
postures my body.

15. choices

he promised
the next needle
would be a depiction
of surrender.

the stitches started
to appear.
i doubted my vision.
he was strong enough
to hold onto this life
embroidery
and all.

we made choices.
his to let go,
and mine to
trace my fingers
over this design.

he made choices
that took all of mine.

i fashioned myself
into a facsimile

of your tapestry.
i chose
the tatters too.

my choice
is an abstract
of surrender.

16. steps

to flourish
means one foot
in front of the other
away
from birthday plans
never realized.

to wilt
is to yearn
as a woman
with your name
crawling from her bed
in the morning
warming up her voice
to practice laughter.

to decay
is to remember
the embraces
and closed fists
and let the weight
of what is carried
scatter to the ground
around your knees.

to honor
it seems
is some unbearable
combination
of the three.

to survive
is to stand still
around any of it.

17. two footprints

you were a boy once,
barefoot and toddling,
trouble
from the first steps.

you were a boy once,
whale rides
sister on your back
in the pool,
before
gunpowder and smoke.

you were a man once,
before you knew what that was
filling shoes
you struggled to tie.

you were a man once,
running
from the boy
you were,
consumed
by the fog
and sacrificing him

for it.

you were a man once,
bearing the weight
of a wife
to hold her upright,
lacing the shoes
you once stumbled in.

you were a man once,
baby girl on your shoulders
gently slipping
glass slippers onto
her feet.

and more than anything
you were every step
of my way.

18. paper swans

scattered around the house
were a thousand paper swans
made of sticky notes,
index cards,
hymnal pages,
and origami paper.
they came from envelopes
and shrouded gestures,
sometimes just appearing
on countertops and nightstands.

packed into
my bedside drawers
are a thousand letters
professing desire,
gratitude,
and desperation.
they often went
unanswered
but i brought them
everywhere i went.

love was the exchange
of knowing glances,

the lunches left in the fridge,
the early morning coffee,
"i love you"s written in
paper swans
that could never float
in water.

19. ants

he stares out,
palm pressed
against the window
in silence.
there are ants
down below
dots gathered around
what he assumes
to be a stone.
they stand frozen
for some time.
then he observes
a splintered line
receding.

they stand gathered
heads turning
searching
for a soul or a sign.
some arms reach
for the heavens
some insist
from there
he is looking.

he was bigger
than any mountain,
any building
ever seen.
he was their everything.

20. rip currents

your mother dreamed of
some island vacation.
you told me before,
you were afraid of the water.
she recounted stories
of you swimming
in the ocean
and fishing
with your grandfather.
i wonder what marred
those memories.

buried in your arms
ice water ran down my back.
i already knew
these pinpoint pupils
and the dewdrops in your eyes.
i didn't want or need the admission.

i needed to understand.
i offer my arm.
you find a vein
and suddenly i'm underwater.

the salt stings my eyes
as i try to get my bearings.
miles above me,
your lonely silhouette,
heads in your hands.
far above me
the sun's rays
are breaking through the surface.
there's a peace
that comes
over drowning victims
moments before death.
you would tell me one day
that you didn't know
how else to stop
my pain.
all at once,
i realize why
you were afraid of the water.

21. responsibility

first came may,
the month i was
too hard on him.
then came june
when i didn't have
enough discernment.
july passed, and
this was my fault.
in august,
it was the disease.
for september,
it was his fault.

october came
with the realization;
i should've stayed up that night.
throughout november,
it was the act
of a vengeful god.
in december,
he's gone because
he ran out of chances.

each month that passes

is a step away from your grave.
for january,
i pray,
there is nothing left
to blame.

www.ingramcontent.com/pod-product-compliance
Lightning Source LLC
Chambersburg PA
CBHW061724130726

47996CB00006B/2486